Dealing With Debt

Dr Andy Hill

Dedication

To all those who have helped me during the many times I have been in debt.

Introduction

I have worked in the IT industry for all my working life. Either being self employed or working for small companies.

At the tender age of 46 I suffered a stroke and have not been able to work full time since.

All of this combined with my poor money management skills, has led me into flirting with debt on several occasions.

Although debt is not a good situation to be in, it is far from the end of the world!

This book lists a few tricks for dealing with debt that moat people don't know about and the banks and other institutions don't want you to know about.

This book is true for English law, but similar principles should apply in other countries as well. However you are advised to check your local laws before proceeding.

Please also note that I am no legal expert and I cannot take any responsibilities for any problems you may encounter following the procedures suggested in this book. It is intended as a guide only and carries no legal standing.

Chapter 1 – Getting into Debt

By far the best way of dealing with debt is not to get into it in the first place! Always try to live within your means, try to build up some "rainy day" savings and always have at least a months wages in reserve to cover any unexpected bills.

Often however, this ideal situation cannot be achieved. Through illness, family tragedy, loss of job or as so often in my case, just downright bad planning.

So once you've managed to get into debt for whatever reason, what should you do?

Firstly don't panic!

As with most of life's problems early action can prevent the problem from escalating.

If you just have one missed payment to one creditor, contact them, let them know what is going on and when you expect to make the payment.

Better still contact them as soon as you know you are likely to miss the payment.

They are obliged by law to help you to avoid getting into financial difficulties.

If you have missed payments, or expect to miss payments to several creditors, contact them all as described above.

So dealing with the issue early should present you with minimal problems, a single late or missed payment to one or more creditors can be dealt with quickly and easily simply by talking to your creditor(s).

What if you cash flow problem is more serious and you are likely to miss more than one payment or simply cannot afford to make certain payments for a period of time?

Don't Panic! You can still resolve the situation by talking to your creditors.

Whatever happens, you must talk to your creditors, you can't just ignore the problem and hope it will go away.

If you ignore your creditors they will assume that you are trying to get away without paying the debt and they will try ever increasingly strong measures to get their money back.

So again talk to your creditors, make an agreed repayment schedule (See Chapter 3) that you can afford, for unsecured loans they will almost certainly accept this. Even for secured loans, the lender will usually prefer to come to an arrangement rather than go down the repossession route.

Once you have made a repayment agreement it is important that you stick to it, otherwise you will again be in breach of your credit agreement. Again if you are having problems or think you are going to have problems, then speak to your creditors rather than ignoring the situation and hoping it will go away.

Chapter 2 – Things you probably don't know about debt

Banks and other financial institutions don't want you to know too much about debt, as this would lessen their power over you.

Although they have a duty of care, to help you if you get into debt, initially they don't let you know this. I guess they do this to try to ward off people who are just trying to get out of the debt or think they can just get away with missing payments.

All licensed lenders have to adhere to a code of practice, which covers the procedures they must follow when people get into difficulties with their payments.

(At this point it is worth saying that you should never get involved with unlicensed lenders, the so called loan sharks. As these are not covered by any such codes of practice, in fact their response to you getting behind on payments is likely to be threatening you with physical harm!)

If you are genuinely having financial difficulties and not just trying to get out of paying your debts, then any licensed creditor is obliged to help you and not force you into an increasingly desperate situation.

All creditors accept that you and your family have to live and enjoy the odd treat. They will not however tolerate you living a life of luxury whilst claiming you cannot afford your repayments.

Whether you have one or several creditors, you should draw up a cash flow plan (see Chapter 3), this will show how much money you have left after your priority bills (see Chapter 3), which should then be divided up proportionately between your debtors (see Chapter 3).

Once you have a repayment agreement set up your creditor will suspend interest and any other charges.

However if you miss one of your agreed payments, the agreement will be cancelled and interest and other charges will again be applied. Once again it is important to speak to your creditors and let them know what is happening, providing you can make the missed payment within 2 weeks for a monthly agreement or one week for a fortnightly agreement they will usually keep the agreement going, it is important though that the next scheduled payment is made on time.

If your circumstances change for the better you should re-contact your creditors and agree increased payments by drawing up a new cash flow plan. This is an act of good will on your part and will stand you in good stead for any late payments or renegotiations should your circumstances change for the worse.

Similarly if you circumstances for the worse, you should contact you creditors, draw up a new cash flow plan and agree new payment amounts.

One important thing to note at this point is that any credit defaults will be shown on your credit records but if you have an agreed repayment schedule this will count in your favour. Also when you repay the finance at the end of your repayment, the default will be removed from your credit record.

The reason why creditors will agree to these repayment plans is that if they took you to court, which would cost them money, and you presented the court with the same cash flow plan, the court would be likely to agree to lower repayments. They would also be unlikely to ask you to pay the full court costs.

There are also more formal agreements that you can come up with like creditors voluntary agreements or CVAs (see Chapter 3) these usually involve a third party and will cost you money in some charges, but these do take all the dealing with your creditors out of your hands and all that you will have to do is make a single monthly payment and the third party will do the rest, of course they make a charge for this which will be added to your monthly payment.

The ultimate formal agreement is bankruptcy (see Chapter 3). This should only be used as a last resort as it means you completely lose control of your finances, which are handled by an administrator. Also bankruptcy stays on your record for at least 7 years and there are many things you cannot do until your bankruptcy is discharged, at the end of the repayments.

The advantage of bankruptcy however is that you will usually only pay 30-70% or your total debts.

Bankruptcy is expensive for you, unless it is issued by one of your creditors, which again they will usually only use as a last resort.

So as you can see if you do manage to get into debt it is important to talk to your creditors.

Another important thing about debt is that creditors are not allowed to threaten you in any way.

Which is why they use phrases like it is not in your best interests to run your account in this way. Although under English law it is considered a threat to even say if <something> then <something> will happen. So in my opinion for a creditor to say "If you do not make a payment then we will take other action they recover the money", could be considered as a threat.

If you feel you are being threatened by a creditor you should tell them, as this will worry them knowing they are not allowed to do this.

Equally though you cannot threaten them either, so you can't say "If you don't stop threatening me, then I won't pay".

If you are really lucky, if you maintain a payment plan a creditor may write off at least part of the debt..

Chapter 3 – Tools and Terminology

In this chapter I explain some of the tools and terminology relating to debt.

Cash Flow Plan

This is a simple document, can be a spreadsheet, which lists all your incoming money in one column and all your priority payments (see below) in the other column.

This should be done for a pay period, monthly or weekly, depending on how you are paid.

Both columns are totalled and the Priority payments total subtracted from the Incoming total to give the amount of money available to pay your creditors. This available amount is then allocated proportionately (see below) to all of your creditors.

Example cash flow plan

Incomings	Priority Payments	Income – priority payments
Wages 1000	Rent 350	
	Council tax 100	
	Utilities 100	
	Food 100	
	Petrol 50	
	Mobile 30	
Total 1000	730	270

This is not a brilliant example as I have missed out things like clothes, kids dinner money and other sundries. Make sure you include all of your essential outgoings.

Priority Bills (payments)

These are payments that must be made in order to live.

They include but are not limited to

Rent / Mortgage Payments

Food

Clothes

Petrol / bus/ Train fares

Children's dinner money / school club costs

Council tax

Gas & Electricity

Water bills

Telephone / mobile / internet

Proportional creditor payments

Your creditors will expect to be paid in proportion to the amount that you owe them. The ones that you owe the most to will expect a bigger slice of the cake than those you only owe a little to.

For example if your cash flow plan shows you have £270 left over each month and you have 3 creditors that you owe as follows.

Creditor1	2000	74%
Creditor2	500	18%
Creditor3	200	8%
Total	2770	

Then you need to work out the proportion of the total that is owed to each creditor.

You do this as Amount owed to Creditor / Total Amount owed *100

So for Creditor1 2000 / 2770 * 100 = 74 (rounded off)

So then to work out how much you need to pay each creditor

Amount Available * (proportion / 100)

So for Creditor1 in the above example

270 * (74 /100) = £200 (rounded off)

Creditor2

270 * (18 /100) = £49 (rounded off)

and Creditor3 gets what is left over. £21

If your outgoings are greater than your incomings or the amount of money left after priority bills is insignificant. You should offer a token payment of £1 per month to each creditor until your situation improves.

Creditor's Voluntary Agreement

Or more particularly relating to an individual, an Individual Voluntary Agreement.

*n England and Wales, an **individual voluntary arrangement** (IVA) is a formal alternative for individuals wishing to avoid bankruptcy.*

The IVA was established by and is governed by Part VIII of the Insolvency Act 1986 and constitutes a formal repayment proposal presented to a debtor's creditors via an insolvency practitioner. Usually (but not necessarily), the IVA comprises only the claims of unsecured creditors, leaving the rights of secured creditors largely unchanged. Insolvency practitioners charge initial and ongoing fees that are in addition to the debt.

An IVA is a contractual arrangement with creditors and can be as flexible as an individual's own circumstances; they can therefore be based on capital, income, third party payments or a combination of these.

In this process, a debtor who has enough money left over after priority creditors and essential expenses, may be able to arrange an individual voluntary arrangement.[1] (After taking independent advice, debtors with less serious problems may wish to consider a debt management plan).

The analogous procedure for businesses is the company voluntary arrangement. (1)

This is simply a more formalised version of our debt management plan previously discussed.

Bankruptcy

This is the ultimate form of debt management, where complete control of your financial affairs is handed over to an administrator.

Should only be used as a last resort.

Bankruptcy *is a legal status of a person or <u>other entity</u> that cannot repay the debts it owes to <u>creditors</u>. In most jurisdictions, bankruptcy is imposed by a <u>court order</u>, often initiated by the <u>debtor</u>.*

Bankruptcy is not the only legal status that an insolvent person or other entity may have, and the term bankruptcy is therefore not a synonym for <u>insolvency</u>. In some countries, including the <u>United Kingdom</u>, bankruptcy is limited to individuals, and other forms of insolvency proceedings (such as <u>liquidation</u> and <u>administration</u>) are applied to companies. In the United States, bankruptcy is applied more broadly to formal insolvency proceedings.(2)

Agreed Repayment Schedule

This is the agreement between you an your creditors as to how much and how often will be paid towards your debt.

Either party may request a review of this from time to time.

Chapter 4 – Conclusions

The best way to deal with debt is not to get into it in the first place!

Always try to live within your means and try to build up some rainy day savings of at least a months wages.

If you do get into debt, don't panic, don't start getting payday loans and loans from loan sharks.

Talk to you creditors, if it is a one off hiccup they will often let you miss a payment or make up for it later, as long as they know about it.

If it is a longer term problem, draw up a cash flow and send it to all your creditors along with your payment proposals.

You can get other companies to do this for you along with the more formal Individual Voluntary Agreement, however these options will cost you more money. As a final option there is always Bankruptcy.

Once you have an agreement in place you must stick to it. If you are still having problems, again talk to your creditors and agree on a more manageable arrangement.

Don't be afraid of being taken to court, as long as the court can see you are making every effort to pay, they will not penalise you further. If fact they will often agree more manageable terms for you.

Creditors will often use the threat of court but back down when you call their bluff and say "OK take me to court".

Finally, once you have cleared your debts, try your hardest to avoid the same situation in the future.

Acknowledgements

(1) From Wikipedia, the free encyclopedia

(2) From Wikipedia, the free encyclopedia